Dropped-D Tuning For Fingerstyle Guitar

By Tom Ball

Acknowledgments:

CD recorded primarily at Riviera Studio (Santa Barbara CA) Wayne Sabbak, engineer
also at:
Sage Arts Studio (Arlington WA) Daniel Protheroe, engineer
Songdog Studio (Santa Barbara CA) John O'Connor, engineer
Goldmine Studio (Ventura CA) John Koenig, engineer
JER Studio (Santa Barbara CA) Juan Esparza, engineer
Songwriters and Musicians Studio (Santa Barbara CA) Jim Shaffer, engineer.

Mastered to CD by Wayne Sabbak at Riviera Studio, Santa Barbara CA

A lot of folks helped to put this together.
In addition to those named above, the author would also like to thank:

Laurie Linn Ball, Folk Mote Music, Shanynn Raigh, Kenny Sultan,
Danny "Bassharp" Wilson, Tom Stapleton, the Mercer Group, and my family.

Thank you one and all!

Cover design – Jim Filippi
Layout – Kenny Warfield
Production – Ron Middlebrook

ISBN 1-57424-123-0
SAN 683-8022

Young Folklorist (interviewing Joseph Spence in the early 1970's:) Mr. Spence, I couldn't help noticing that you play all your songs in the same tuning, dropped-D tuning, and the same key, D major. Why is that?

Spence: I used to know all them keys! I knew 'em all: A, and B, and D, and F, and H... I used to know all them keys!

YF: Well Mr. Spence, if that's true, then why do you play everything in the same key of D? Why don't you use any of those other keys?

Spence: I got tired of 'em!

Joseph Spence.

"Dropped-D? What you talkin' 'bout? Oh, you mean "Po' Boy Tuning!""
-Sam Chatmon

About The Author

Although he is perhaps better known as the singing/harmonica-playing half of the blues and ragtime partnership he has with Kenny Sultan, Tom Ball is also a steel string guitarist of no small import. Based in Santa Barbara, Tom and Kenny play concerts, clubs and festivals all over the world. In addition to his duo work, Tom has well over 100 CD credits on harmonica and/or guitar, including his solo guitar CD "Guitar Music" (Fantasy KM-CD 3906.) The duo has a total of eight instructional books with Centerstream as well as nine albums, most of which are available either on Flying Fish/Rounder or on No Guru.

For information on Tom's other books "Blues Harmonica," "The Nasty Blues," "A Sourcebook of Sonny Terry Licks," "A Sourcebook of Little Walter/Big Walter Licks," and/or the upcoming "A Sourcebook of Sonny Boy Williamson I & II Licks," write: Centerstream Publishing, P.O. Box 17878, Anaheim Hills, CA 92807 USA or email: centerstrm@aol.com

For info on Tom & Kenny's latest duo recording, write: No Guru Entertainment, P.O. Box 8351, Van Nuys CA 91409 or email: nogururecords@aol.com For info on most of Tom & Kenny's other duo recordings, write: Rounder Records, One Camp Street, Cambridge, MA 02140 USA, or access: www.rounder.com

For info on Tom's solo guitar recording, access: www.fantasy.com (As this goes to press, Tom's second solo guitar CD is being recorded.)

For correspondence with the author:
Tom Ball, P.O. Box 20156, Santa Barbara, CA 93120 USA,
Or access: www.tomballkennysultan.com

Tom Ball.

4

Table Of Contents

Introduction

What's so special about dropped-D Tuning? It's almost exactly like standard tuning, isn't it?

Well, yes and no. On the face of it, dropped-D tuning couldn't be much simpler: you've only to drop your bass string down two frets from E to D (resulting in D A D G B E, bass to top.) So why is it that this humble variation has so much application in guitar music - so many fans, if you will, amongst both guitarists and (probably oblivious) listeners?

The answer lies within the sound itself. The next time you watch an accomplished guitarist test out a instrument in a shop, keep an eye open: chances are within five minutes the player will have tuned the bass down to D for a few moments, testing out the sonority and sympathetic "beating" of the instrument's D-chord. A player can learn much about an instrument's integrity from this simple exercise: the degree of "decay" within its resonance, the (inevitable) traces of intonation problems (primarily on the first and second strings,) and the overall cooperation of timbre between the three bass strings. Nothing makes a guitar ring like a dropped-D.

This particular tuning lends itself well to almost any type of music: folk, classical, blues, Irish, new age, Latin, etc. It is particularly well suited for slower pieces, which take full advantage of the tuning's resonant characteristics. Much of the material written in dropped-D could be described as "stately" or "elegant." The simplicity and grace within this tuning are the elements that catch one's ear, (and hopefully one's spirit.)

For this project I've selected 17 pieces in dropped-D tuning, covering a wide array of musical genres. All are played fingerstyle, which is with the thumb and finger(s) of the right hand. If you are a flat-picker, this probably isn't the book for you!

Most fingerstyle players use the thumb and first two fingers of the right hand, though some use more. Your instructor is something of a dinosaur in that I only use the thumb and index finger, a picking style I seem to be stuck with but would not recommend. On the accompanying CD I am using a thumbpick and one steel fingerpick, but they're not really necessary - I'll leave those decisions up to you.

With the exception of the spoken introduction (and the two bonus tracks,) the accompanying CD is much the same as any other commercial guitar recording - there are no intrusive comments, tips or instructions on the CD. Instead, such instructions are found within the written pages of this book. In doing it this way, it is my hope that the CD can also double as a guitar recording, and (with luck) be enjoyed on it's own by non-guitarists and others who may not have a specific interest in actually learning to play the pieces.

Warning to purists: musical liberties have been taken with these! Although the arrangements are close, there is no attempt here to play, for example, a Blind Blake piece precisely 100% like Blake did it; first of all nobody can play like Blake, but more importantly I think it's a more valuable lesson to make any piece one's own. My recommendation would be that once you learn a piece from this (or any other) book, change it, mix it up, and vary upon it. Have fun and make it your own! Music is meant to be about expression and enjoyment, not necessarily about slavishly playing everything exactly as written.

Finally, it is my fervent wish that guitarists and listeners might use this project as a jumping off point to explore and appreciate the many masters of dropped-D Tuning, from Augustin Barrios to Joseph Spence, and Ry Cooder to Leo Brouwer. The legacy of their works is a precious one for all lovers of the guitar.

Ry Cooder.

The Earliest Solo (and Dropped-D) Guitar Recordings

In the liner notes to **John Williams - Barrios** (Columbia M-35145) no less an authority than Mr. Williams himself is quoted as saying: "(Augustin Barrios) was the first guitarist to make recordings, beginning in 1909." Another source, the notes to **Nick Lucas: The Singing Troubadour** (AJA 5022,) has Michael Pitts making the same claim for Lucas, stating that Lucas "recorded for Pathe the first guitar solo record ever made..."

Recent research however, (notably Tim Gracyk's essay in Victrola And 78 Journal no. 3) indicates that both these sources are incorrect and that at least two other guitarists predated both Barrios and Lucas.

"Octaviano Yanes," writes Gracyk, "appears to have recorded solo pieces... for Edison in Mexico City around March to May 1907." Of interest to guitarists perusing this volume, at least some of the Yanes pieces utilized alternate tunings and/or instruments. Quoting Gracyk again, "(On **Habaneres**) Yanes plays an instrument with at least seven strings. From low to high note it is tuned B E A D B B E.

"Dick Spottswood also identified two solo guitar performances recorded in Havana, Cuba for Edison by Sebastian Hidalgo," Gracyk continues. "These cylinders... would have been recorded in late 1905 to March 1906, so these are arguably the first guitar solos. Does anyone own copies? We cannot rule out the possibility of earlier solo guitar recordings made in Europe."

And so the search continues! As we shall see in a short later discussion of Barrios, Mr. Williams has misdated Barrios' recording debut by a bit, but until the missing Hidalgo and Yanes recordings surface it will be impossible to pinpoint either the first solo guitar recordings or the first dropped-D tuned recordings.

What is known, however, is that Augustin Barrios actually began recording sometime between 1910 and 1913 in Uruguay, and that the first piece he recorded in dropped-D was **La Paloma** (Atlanta 65.36 H7, recorded 1913.) I will go out on a limb then, and suggest that **La Paloma** (written by Yradier) may well be the first solo guitar piece ever recorded in dropped-D. Readers are encouraged to please write me with any factual data which my either confirm or contradict this supposition.

In any event, dozens of guitar pieces in dropped-D were recorded in the '20s and early '30s, among them a few in this volume: William Moore's **One Way Gal** (1928,) Blind Blake's somewhat similar **Chump Man Blues** (1929) and Funny Paper Smith's **Hungry Wolf** (1931.)

The point of all this rambling is to say that dropped-D tuning has some history. It's not some new-agey configuration brought to you via the elevator-music guitar clan so popular today. The tuning is probably as old as the instrument itself and has a place in guitar music everywhere.

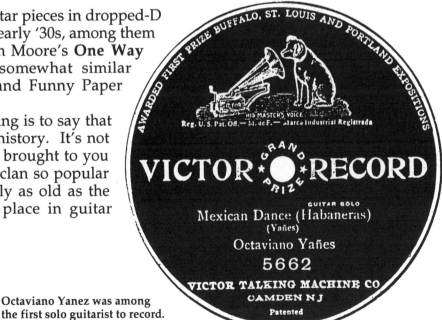

Octaviano Yanez was among the first solo guitarist to record.

Dropped-D Shapes

Although there are exceptions (like the three songs in this book in the key of A,) most tunes in dropped-D are played in the key of D.

The three chords which make up the key of D are: D, A and G. Naturally there are other chords (and variants), which appear, but these are the main three. Since the only difference between dropped-D tuning and standard tuning is the bass string, the only cardinal rule to remember is: when fretting, play the bass string two frets higher than you usually would.

Ordinarily when strumming a D chord in standard tuning, players either avoid the sixth string or perhaps fret it at the second fret (F#.) But now that the bass has been lowered to D, all six strings can be sounded on a D chord (fig. 1.)

When shifting to a G chord, remember that the bass G note will no longer be at the third fret - it's now at the fifth fret. But since an alternating bass pattern is often called for on the right hand, the fifth (A) string can often be avoided altogether, resulting in a simplified G chord shaped like fig. 2. And when you want to finger a G chord which includes the fifth string (but not the sixth,) you can play the shape in fig. 3.

When the song calls for an E chord (or E7 or E minor,) remember that you must now fret the sixth string at the second fret to get your bass E note (fig. 4.)

Many of these songs also call for a D chord with an added third (as in fig. 5.) This chord can feel awkward at first, but don't forget there's a short-cut (cheat) method that you can often use: unless the right hand pattern specifically calls for you to play all four fingered high strings (very rare,) a player can get away with a partial chord (like those in figs. 6 and 7.) These are much easier to land upon and they work fine, provided the picker avoids playing the string(s), which are then left uncovered. (Note the Xs; these mean avoid due to dissonance. Also note the X? Above the first string on figs. 6 and 7; that's because there is no hard-and-fast rule on that particular E note... sometimes you might want it, sometimes not...)

Here's another cheap trick: a lot of these songs call for an A chord, but don't require you to ever actually play the first string. In such a case it's far easier to simply barre the chord with your index finger (fig. 8,) but then you must be careful to avoid playing that high E string altogether (unless, perhaps, you want to add an A on top, as in fig. 9.)

Because of moving bass lines in some pieces, it can be difficult to pin down specific chord positions - due to this movement, an indicated chord might really only refer to the harmonic center of what's going on. Figs. 10-14 show some other useful shapes.

So.... have I confused you?? Good! Now let's play!

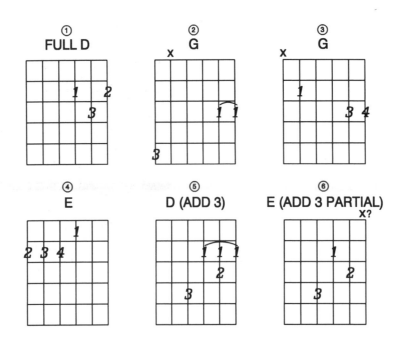

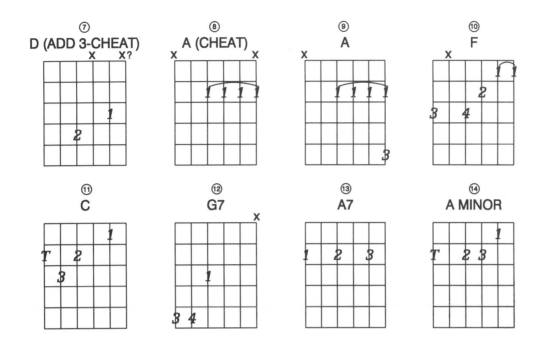

Tom Ball (1973). (Photo by Dick Rudolph)

Explanation Of The Tab

As most of you know, tablature is an incomplete system in that there are no timing indications. I consider it to be simply a system of shorthand, to be used in conjunction either with the standard notation, or with one's own ears via the recorded examples on the CD. In my own case, I can't read standard notation to save my soul, so I am doubly grateful for the fact that so many books are finally surfacing which present pieces in both standard and in tab.

In a nutshell, tablature works like this: there are six lines. Each line indicates a string - i.e. the top line indicates the first (or high-E) string; the second line down indicates the second (or B) string, etc., all the way down to the lowest line, which indicates the low (in this case dropped-D) string.

A number indicates the fretted position. Zero indicates an open string; one indicates the first fret, etc. etc. In most cases the right (or picking) thumb will play the bass notes on the three bass strings, while the finger(s) will ordinarily play on the three treble strings.

A few other oddities to be mentioned include:

1. **The hammer-on:** in the case of a hammer-on, I will indicate it with an "H." If you see something that looks like this: 2H3, it means the second fret is played, then a quick hammer to the third fret is executed with the left hand.

2. **The pull-off:** in the case of a pull-off, it is indicated with a "P." If you see something like this: 2P0, it means the second fret is played, then a quick pull-off to the open string is executed with the left hand.

(In some cases you may see something like this: 2H3P2, which would mean play the second fret, then hammer to the third fret, then pull-off back to the second fret.)

3. **The slide:** Slides are indicated with a dash, i.e. 2-4 would mean to play the second fret, then slide your finger up to the 4th fret.

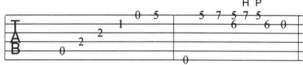

4. **The bend:** When a note is to be bent, it is indicated with a ♪ For example, a 6 means to play the note on the 6th fret, then bend the string up to approximate what it would sound like if you were playing it at the 7th.

5. **The harmonic:** In the case of harmonics, they're indicated by a diamond shaped box around the fret, which should be played as a harmonic. In addition you'll also see the abbreviation "harm."

CD Track Sheet

1. Introduction (1:54)
2. John Hardy (Desperate Man Blues) (1:32)
3. Rake And Ramblin' Boy (1:31)
4. Stack O' Lee (0:48)
5. Comin' In On A Wing And A Prayer (2:46)
6. Face To Face That I Shall Know Him (1:48)
7. Great Dreams Of Heaven (2:46)
8. Hungry Wolf (1:40)
9. Chump Man Blues (0:42)
10. One Way Gal (1:28)
11. Danny Boy (3:40)
12. Maria Elena (2:19)
13. Caribbean Gospel Tune (2:03)
14. 'Bout A Spoonful (0:53)
15. Big Bill Style Blues (1:22)
16. Unknown Title (Folk Song in A/B) (0:58)
17. Berceuse (3:44)
18. Julia Florida (3:35)

19. Bonus Track #1: La Paloma (recorded 1913) (2:50). As stated elsewhere, I believe that La Paloma, written by Yradier and played by Augustin Barrios may well be the first solo guitar recording ever made in dropped-D tuning. It was recorded in Uruguay in 1913, and released on the Atlanta label (65.367.)

20. Bonus Track #2: Bad Feeling Blues (recorded 1927). Bad Feeling Blues by Blind Blake was waxed in Chicago in May of 1927, and released on Paramount 12497. Along with Chump Man Blues, it is one of the few tunes Blake played in dropped-D. I hope you'll like it. Incidentally, the following advertisement ran in the Chicago Defender in 1927:

11

Traditional Folk Songs

There are an infinite number of traditional folk songs that work well in dropped-D. Let's take a look at three of them.

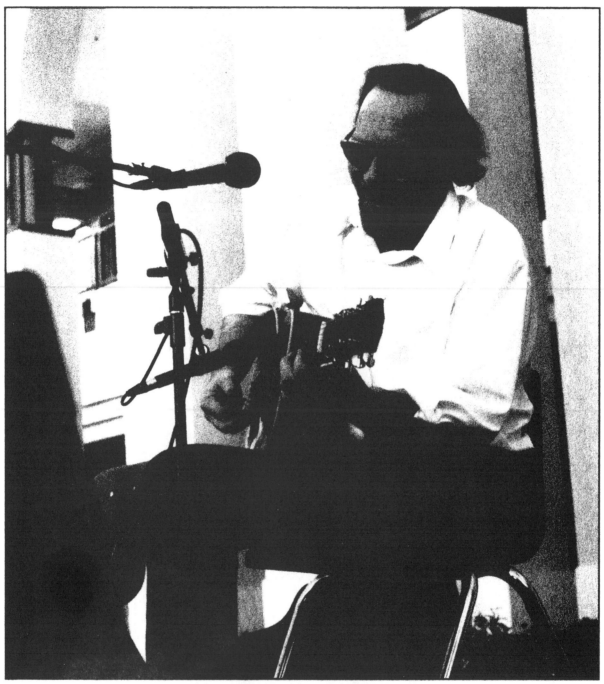

Tom Ball. (Photo by Ben Elder)

Tom Ball belongs to the one or two guitars is good enough for me club. Tom found his sunburst finish Gibson PG-00 (Plectrum Guitar, it was a four-string version on an L-00 body, the L standing for guitarist Nick Lucas), about 20 years ago. Although the craggy instrument has no serial number, he says, "The consensus among people who've looked at it is that it's a 1936."

He had luthier Jim Lombard make a new neck and belly bridge to replace the undersize original parts. Undersize parts aren't all bad, though; Tom likes the lighter top bracing designed for original four strings. Lombard also retained the original, Gibson-logo peghead veneer and fashioned a curious fretmarker pattern. The fingerboard inlays are flowers and diamonds, with a tenth-fret fingerboard marker trand a ninth-fret side dot. This mismatched arrangement mirrors the pattern on a '20s-era Washburn parlor guitar tom has owned for decades. "I asked Jim to do it this way, he explains, "because it's what I'm used to looking at."

John Hardy
(aka Desperate Man Blues)

We'll start off with one of the first folk songs I learned to fingerpick in dropped-D. It employs a very straightforward alternating bass (Travis style) picking pattern. The left hand here is actually very simple; throughout most of the song the left ring finger remains anchored on the second string, third fret.

The most unusual and engaging aspect of this pattern is that the melody line is carried by the bass and not the treble, and mostly via hammer-ons.

Rake And Ramblin' Boy

Another traditional folk song, this one has a little trickier bass line, which descends firstly on the bass (sixth) string, and then on the fifth. There are three verses of this on the CD, all of which are pretty similar; here's the (6 measure) intro, plus the first two (16 measure) verses:

14

VERSE 2

15

Stack O'Lee

Continuing in the folk tradition, this arrangement of the old war-horse **Stack O'Lee** owes a bit to each of Mississippi John Hurt, Doc Watson and Taj Mahal. Please note the use of a capo on the second fret, resulting in the true key of E.

Joseph Spence Style

Of all the guitarists profiled in this volume (and for that matter, of all the guitarists profiled **anywhere**,) Joseph Spence is the only one I know of who played **exclusively** in dropped-D. His approach to guitar was utterly unique, and it is hoped that students of the instrument will seek out and devour his many recordings.

For those who are unfamiliar, Joseph Spence was born in 1910 on Andros Island in the Bahamas. As a child he taught himself guitar, and spent his early years on Andros as a sponge fisherman. By the time he reached adulthood the sponges were nearly extinct, so he moved to Nassau and became a stonemason.

It wasn't until 1958 that he was first recorded, when Sam Charters unexpectedly came across him on Andros. The remarkable tapes of that meeting were soon issued on Folkways Records, and before long Spence had gained himself a small but rabid following in the United States.

A few trips to the U.S. ensued and several more albums were cut (on Nonesuch, Elektra, Arhoolie and Rounder,) but for my money it is the early Folkways material, which really catches Spence at the top of his form. Fortunately these recordings have now been reissued on CD (**The Complete Folkways Recordings** - Smithsonian Folkways CD SF 40066.) Joseph Spence passed away in 1984.

Spence's actual playing style can be as deceptively difficult as it is idiosyncratic. Except for Ry Cooder and the young Bahamian Japheth Dean, most guitarists (myself included) have a hard time getting beyond the mechanics and melodies and into the free rhythm, timing and natural exuberance of his highly individual playing. There is little attempt here to "play it just like Spence..." Almost nobody can!

Although he quickly made each song his own, most of Spence's pieces are adapted from hymns, Bahamian folk songs, and/or the occasional American tin-pan-alley song. For this volume, I've selected three traditional songs long associated with Spence:

Joseph Spence.

Comin' In On A Wing And A Prayer

In addition to Spence's recording of it, Ry Cooder has also done a wonderful ensemble job with **Wing And A Prayer**. The version here starts with a quick and easy 8-bar intro (duly transcribed,) followed by a slow verse lasting about 30 seconds. Because that slow verse consists of essentially the same shapes that appear later, it is not transcribed.

The up tempo stuff is the meat of the song, and the first 16 measure up-tempo verse played on the CD is what follows here. Also included is the tricky 4 bar lick which is located about 90 seconds into the piece.

The slow outro is excluded due to redundancy, but if you're interested in the harmonic-laden ending, please refer to the transcription of **Julia Florida**. The two endings are virtually identical, and it is transcribed for you there.

Words and Music by Jimmy McHugh and Harold Adamson

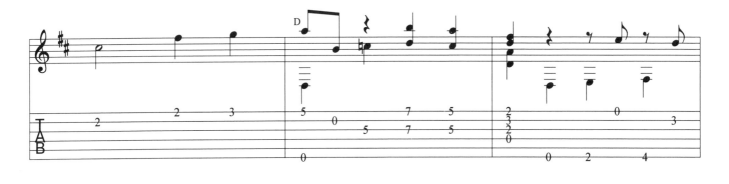

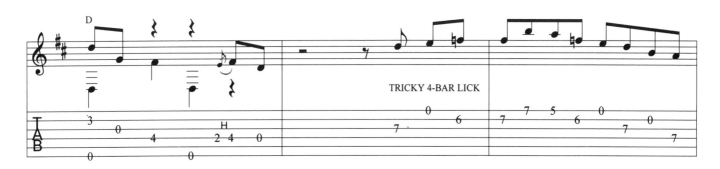

TRICKY 4-BAR LICK

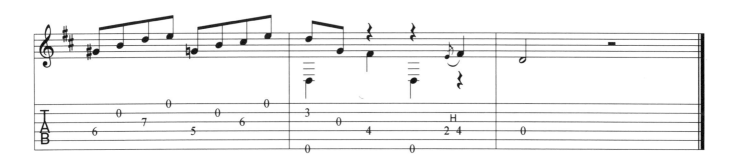

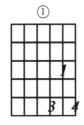

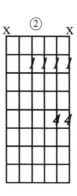

19

Face To Face That I Shall Know Him

Here's an old gospel piece that Spence played. It's very **direct** - sounds almost like a march!

My recording of this is made up of 5 (16 bar) verses, but there's really only two parts, an A section and a B section which alternate as follows: A, B, A, B, A. The transcription includes both of these sections.

Tom Ball (1979). (Photo by Brian Hugli)

Great Dreams Of Heaven

The first thing you'll notice about this waltz is that it's recorded with the capo at the third fret, resulting in the true key of F.

This is a fun song to play - not particularly difficult. In general the right thumb plucks the bass (in 3/4 time) by striking the open sixth string once, followed by the open fourth string twice.

There are three basic (16 bar) sections to this piece: for simplicity, let's call them A, B and C. Breaking down the structure of the CD version we find that it's set up thusly: A, A, B, C, A, A, B, A.

For the transcription that follows, first comes the A section (or first verse;) then the B section (or third verse;) and finally the C section (or fourth verse.)

22

The Blues

Unknown 12 String Bluesman

Unknown String Band

Blind Lemon Jefferson

Blind Blake

Lonnie Johnson

Blind Willie McTell

Memphis Minnie
& Kansas Joe

Big Bill Broonzy

Rev. Gary Davis

Blind Boy Fuller

Blues In D

First up: please note that while my transcriptions of these pieces capture the essence, melody and basic changes of the songs, they are not intended to be 100% dead-on note-for-note transcriptions. Rather they are to be considered "in the style of" the artists in question.

Having said that, while D may not be the most common guitar key for blues, it can be used quite effectively if the bass string is dropped down to a D note.

In terms of early regional guitar characteristics, dropped-D could fit in anywhere and nowhere: as a generalization, early Texas-based blues guitarists seemed to prefer the keys of E and A; Piedmont and East Coast pickers leaned heavily toward C and G; and Delta players tended toward slide guitar in the open tunings (primarily open G and open D.) Still, dropped-D blues popped up now and then in all the regions, and to great effect. Let's look at three early examples:

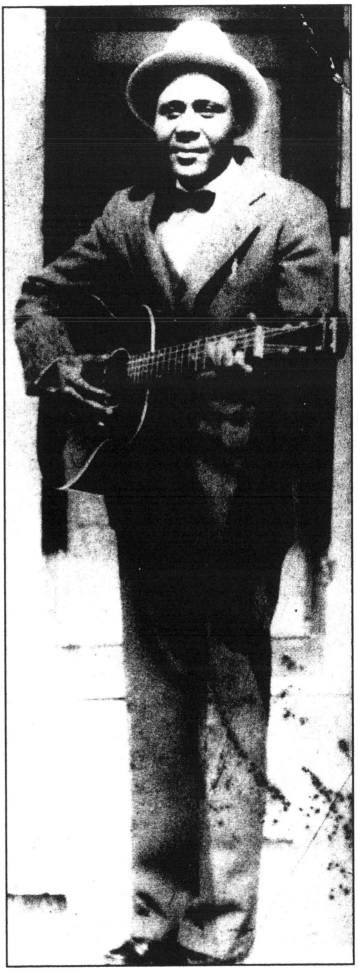

J.T. Smith.

Funny Paper Smith's Hungry Wolf

J. T. Smith was a significant if relatively unknown Texas-style guitarist and blues singer, whose short recording career began and ended in the early 1930's. Alternately billed as "Funny Paper Smith" and "The Howling Wolf" (not to be confused with Chester Burnett, the latter-day Chicago blues artist who also used the alias "Howlin' Wolf,") he recorded 20 sides for Vocalion before his career was short-circuited by a murder conviction in 1931.

Hungry Wolf is one of the few pieces Smith recorded in D; he usually preferred the more common Texas keys of A and E. Like most Texas players he often opted for a monotone thump bass, whereas on this song he comes close to an alternating bass. It must be mentioned that Smith actually played this in standard tuning with the bass string at it's normal E, but I think it works better with the bass down to D. On the Yazoo reissue LP of this (**"Funny Papa Smith: The Original Howling Wolf, 1930-1931"**) either the recording was mastered one half-step sharp to pitch or Smith was tuned that way; but in either case, playing along with Smith's version necessitates a capo at the first fret. On this book's accompanying CD I am playing it without a capo. J.T. Smith was an interesting guitarist whose work deserves far greater recognition.

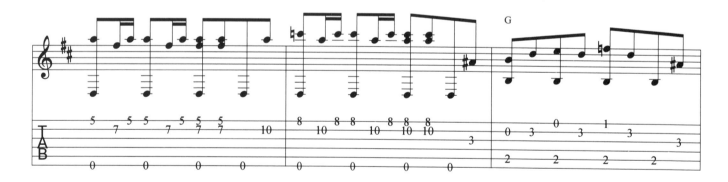

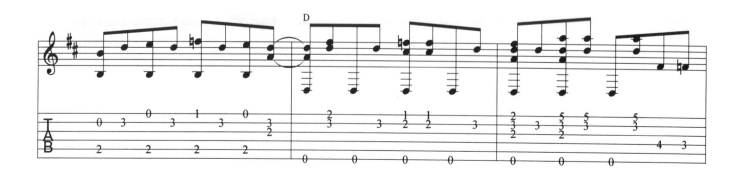

Blind Blake's Chump Man Blues

In terms of both ability and popularity, Blind Blake was without question the preeminent ragtime and blues guitarist of the 1920's. Hailing from Jacksonville, Florida, Blake (r. n. either Arthur Blake or Arthur Phelps) began a successful recording career in 1926 when he waxed the rag tour-de-force **West Coast Blues.**

Over the next six years Blind Blake recorded 79 of his own titles and appeared as a sideman on scores of other recordings. His guitar virtuosity is evidenced by a complete command of nearly all keys and various tunings, although arguably his finest output may have been his stunning rags in the key of C.

Chump Man Blues is something of an oddity for Blake - one of his few excursions into dropped-D (although his **Bad Feeling Blues** is also in the tuning, and **Police Dog Blues** shows his remarkable ability in Open-D.) Please note that this is recorded with the capo at the second fret (resulting in the key of true E,) and that the first verse utilizes what is often half-time bass; somewhat reminiscent of later recordings by Joseph Spence. The second verse is the doubled-up bass.

Although Blake's life is shrouded in mystery and obscurity, his recorded legacy continues to inspire and amaze present day guitarists and fans alike.

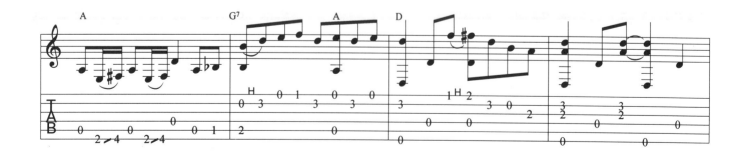

Blind Blake.

29

William Moore's One Way Gal

William Moore's guitar artistry stands in marked contrast to the dearth of information about him. Some sources have him born in Georgia, some in Virginia, but in either case he grew up in Tappahannock, Virginia, and became a barber. In January of 1928 he was picked up by a roving Paramount A&R man who took him to Chicago for a recording session. Though musically superb, the resulting four 78s nevertheless sold poorly and all are exceedingly rare today - **78 Quarterly** estimates that even the most common of them survives in quantities of less than 15 copies.

Never to record again, Moore returned home and resumed his barbering career, moving to Warsaw and later, Warrenton. Elderly citizens of the area still recall him as a fiddler/pianist/guitarist/farmer/barber who lived out his remaining years with his son. He died sometime in the early '50s.

William Moore's light and complex guitar style is typical of the Piedmont region, and often employs alternating-bass and other characteristic ragtime elements. All eight of his recorded pieces are very well played and worth study, but most are in standard tuning and therefore outside the scope of this volume. Paramount ledgers suggest that Moore also recorded eight other tunes at his one and only session, but none of them were issued. Does anyone have test pressings?

On **One Way Gal** Moore starts out sliding up to a strange chord that can only be described as G-chord with an A on top. An in addition to the expected I, IV, V, this song also includes an unexpected E7 chord in the progression.

An Irish Tune

I wanted to include at least one Irish tune in this volume -- and what could be more Irish than "**Danny Boy**?" When played as an instrumental this is also known as "**Old Irish Air**," "**Londonderry Air**," and/or the "**Derry Air**" (but be very careful how you pronounce those titles, especially in France.)

The music is credited to Rory Dall O'Cathain who was chief harpist to Hugh O'Neill, the last of the great Gaelic Chieftains (d. 1616.) Incidentally the "London" add on to "Derry" is relatively recent by Irish standards, occurring around 1610, but "Derry" itself is only the Anglicized version of the earlier Gaelic name of the town, "Doire Colmcille." Translated to English, "Doire Colmcille" means "The Oak Wood Of Colmcille." Therefore, since the Gaelic word for 'air' is 'fonn,' perhaps the most accurate name for this piece might be "Fonn Doire Colmcille" (pronounced 'fun deera collumkill.')

In any event, the starting-off point for this arrangement was Takemitsu's treatment of it from his work "Twelve Songs For Guitar." His take on it is similar (if more complex and 'classical.') The arrangement here quickly diverts from Takemitsu's and employs quite different fingerings; in an attempt to take better advantage of the ringing characteristics of steel strings, this version employs more open strings and is therefore a bit more user-friendly for the steel-string player.

(PS: Thank you to my pal Tom Stapleton of Roscrea, County Tipperary, for the historical info above. See you soon, buddy!)

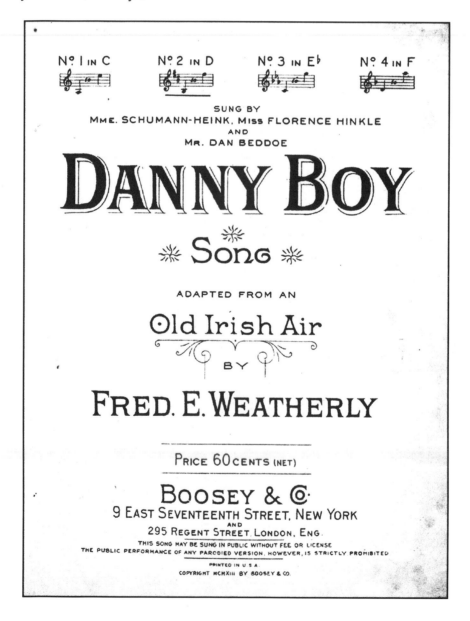

Danny Boy

aka 'Old Irish Air,' 'The Derry Air,' 'Londonderry Air,'
and/or 'Fonn Doire Colmcille.

Dorian Michael.

Latin Pieces

The first of these is **Maria Elena**, and old tin-pan-alley song reputedly written many decades ago as a tribute to the then-first-lady of Mexico. The first thing to note is that on the CD it's played capoed at the second fret, resulting in the true key of E.

The slow first section consists of 32 measures; the upbeat second section is 16 measures plus the repeated ending. The entire arrangement is transcribed.

Maria Elena

Caribbean Gospel Tune

Although I've been playing this one for years, I've never known its' proper name. Stylistically this could fit comfortably amongst the Spence pieces, except that although he seems to have played something similar in live performance, he never recorded it.

On the CD version, the tune starts out slowly for the first 8 measures (almost like a pseudo introduction) before speeding up. Note that on the recording, I'm playing capoed at the first fret resulting in the key of Eb.

REPEAT LAST 4 BARS:
THEN REPEAT FROM THE TOP
UP TO SPEED.............................

Blues And Folk Songs In A

With the exception of the next three tunes, all the pieces in this book are in the key of D (or at least in D-position with a capo.) But as we're about to see, dropped-D can also be a useful tuning for songs played in the key of A.

The two blues which follow have something in common: neither of them employs the alternating-bass pattern found earlier in the "Blues in D" section. Instead they both utilize a thumb-monotone bass, which is solidly in the Texas blues tradition. As a general rule the thumb plucks the fifth (open A) string while on the A chord; it plucks the sixth (open D) while on the D chord; and it plucks the sixth (fretted at the second fret - i.e. an E note) while on the E chord.

Mance Lipscomb. (Photo by Chris Strachwitz)

'Bout A Spoonful

This is played in a pseudo-Mance Lipscomb style. For those who don't know Mance's music, all I can say is rush out and buy some! A wonderful guitarist and an amazing man, Lipscomb was also the subject of Les Blank's great documentary film "A Well Spent Life."

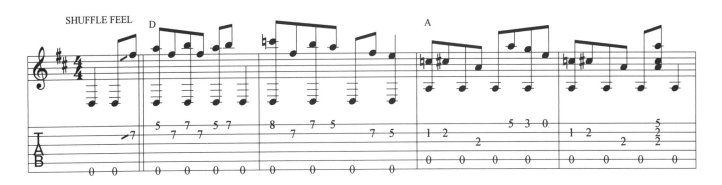

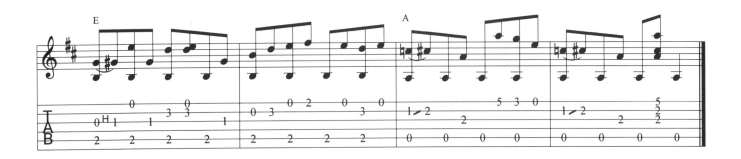

39

Big Bill Style Blues

Big Bill Broonzy was not only a superb guitarist and singer, but also a gifted composer, arranger, organizer, accompanist, storyteller and all-around raconteur. His career was so spectacular that a brief bio does him little justice; his own book **Big Bill Blues** (Da Capo Press) is recommended without reservation.

One of 17 children born to ex-slaves, Broonzy came from Mississippi to Chicago in the '20s and quickly established himself as the premier blues artist in the Windy City. Up until his death in 1958, Big Bill was the most prolific musician in blues history. His output includes an astonishing number of recordings: over 550 in his own name, over 600 more as a sideman. In **Big Bill Blues** Broonzy wrote his own epitaph: "Don't say I'm a musician or guitar player - just write Big Bill was a well known blues singer... he was a happy man when he was drunk and playing with women; he was liked by all the other blues singers."

Big Bill Style Blues is an amalgam of several similar Broonzy pieces in A. I first heard something like this in the mid-'60s, played by my friend John Koenig.

Big Bill Broonzy.

41

Unknown Title
(Folk Song In A/B)

Here's a short and sweet piece that was shown to me by a guitarist who gave me a ride when I was hitchhiking through Mechelen, Belgium in 1969. He never told me the title, but it sounds vaguely Celtic. Although in A position, please note this is capoed at the second fret, resulting in the true key of B. It simply repeats itself; here's a complete verse of it:

FINGERINGS

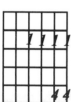

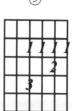
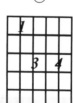
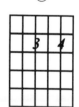

Classical Pieces

The next time you listen to those Segovia or Bream recordings, take notice to see if any of them are played in dropped-D - a surprising percentage of them are!

Berceuse

Cuba's Leo Brouwer is both an astounding composer and a wonderful guitarist. I discovered his playing about 30 years ago with the purchase of the LP **The Classics of Cuba** (Musical Heritage Society 3839,) and have been a fan and student ever since.

Mr. Brouwer's music seems to combine Spanish classical forms with Afro-Cuban folk music and (often atonal) "open forms." On occasion (as in **Espiral Eterna**) his music can be most challenging and difficult to absorb, but this piece is lovely and lush. I am told it is thematically based on the Afro-Cuban lullaby **Drume Negrita**. Note the section at the beginning, which is done by muting the strings with the heel of the right hand.

REPEAT BARS
20 THROUGH 41

45

Julia Florida

I am pleased to conclude this volume with a piece by one of the greatest guitarists of all, Augustin Barrios. Listeners to the accompanying CD have already heard a bit of his playing in the background during the spoken introduction (track one.) As I mentioned then, the complete 1913 Barrios recording of **La Paloma** (which may be the first solo guitar recording ever made in dropped-D,) will follow on the CD as 'bonus track #1.'

Augustin Barrios was gifted in many ways; some might say his greatest work of art was in fact his own life. Any discussion of him must necessarily begin and end with the wonderful Barrios biography **Six Silver Moonbeams** by Richard Stover (Querico Press.) While playing a fine guitar himself, Mr. Stover has also devoted much of his life to resurrecting Barrios' works and to reintroducing Barrios' genius to the masses.

In addition to **Moonbeams**, Stover has also transcribed (in standard notation) the complete works of Barrios and reissued many of his recordings on LP (El Maestro Records.) For years these were the only Barrios reissues available, but I am now pleased to report that a three-CD set entitled **Augustin Barrios - The Complete Guitar Recordings 1913-1942** has become available on the German label Chanterelle Verlag, #CHR 002. While leaving something to be desired in terms of sound quality, this project is arguably the most important guitar reissue to be undertaken in recent years and is highly recommended.

Augustin Pio Barrios (1885-1944) was born in San Juan Bautista, Paraguay, and learned to play guitar as a child. His family valued education and Barrios studied music, mathematics, literature, philosophy and graphic arts at Paraguay's Colegio Nacional before embarking on his career as a solo guitarist.

In 1910 young Barrios left Paraguay for Argentina, then settled in Uruguay where he made a series of solo recordings for the Atlanta and Artigas labels. Ever restless, by 1916 he had moved again, this time to Brazil where he would remain (and record) for 15 years.

Barrios wrote prolifically for solo guitar. He is said to have composed over 300 pieces; of those, over 80 survive in manuscript plus another 60 or so on recordings. His compositions encompass a variety of stylistic influences, from classical to romantic to folklore-inspired dances and mazurkas. His playing itself was dazzling, and all the more so when one considers the limitations of the era's instruments and recording techniques; no editing could be possible, and all were recorded "first take."

Another interesting facet of his playing involved his choice of strings - Barrios used steel strings on the trebles. Good quality gut strings being scarce in South America at the beginning of the century, Augustin strung up with steel. But because he disliked the "twang" of metal strings, he made adjustments by cutting tiny pieces of rubber from pencil erasers and then threading each string through the rubber bits and sliding the rubbers down to meet the saddle of the bridge. In this way the strings' steely response was somewhat dampened, resulting in an unusual and warm tone.

Augustin Barrios.

46

There is no recording of Barrios actually playing his composition that follows, **Julia Florida**. In addition to Julia Florida, he composed at least 23 other pieces in dropped-D, and many more in a similar dropped-D/G tuning (D G D G B E.) The pieces he composed in dropped-D are as follows:

Aire De Zamba *
Ares Andaluzes *
Allegro Sinfonico
Arabescos - Estudio # 4
Cancion de la Hilandera
Capricho Espanol
Cordoba *
Danza
Danza Guarani
Estilo Uruguayo
Estudio del Ligado
Estudio en Sol Menor

Estudio Vals
La Semaratana
Luz Mala *
Minueto en Sol
Oracion *
Pais de Abanico
Pericon *
Preludio - Op. 5, #1
Serenata Morisca
Vals Op.8, #4
Villancico de Navidad

All of these that I have heard are wonderful compositions. The ones that Barrios actually recorded himself are marked with an asterisk (*,) and all are impeccably played. The others survive only in manuscript, although many of them have been recorded by others - most notably either by Richard Stover or John Williams, the latter of whom has said, "Barrios was the greatest guitarist/composer of any time."

Marcha Paraguaya
Célebre Concertista de Guitarra

Augustin P. Barrios
No. 65378.

Augustin Barrios.

Julia Florida

Augustin Barrios

Tom Ball
Harmonica Instruction & Technique

CENTERSTREAM Publishing, LLC - P.O. Box 17878 - Anaheim Hills, CA 92817
714.779.9390 ~ email: centerstrm@aol.com ~ Website: centerstream-usa.com

SOURCEBOOK OF LITTLE WALTER/BIG WALTER LICKS FOR BLUES HARMONICA
by Tom Ball
Centerstream Publishing

In this essential collection for blues harp players, author Tom Ball sets out to discuss, understand and demystify some of the playing of the phenomenal Walters: the legendary "Big Walter" Horton and "Little Walter" Jacobs. Includes a sampling of the best licks from each artist's repertoire, mapped out in easy-to-read harmonica tablature and played on CD by Ball, plus extensive notes on each musician's style, bios and discographies, rare photos, a bibliography, harmonica basics, notes on amplification and equipment, and musch more!
_____00000276 Book/CD Pack.....................$22.95

Blues Harmonica
A COMPREHENSIVE CRASH COURSE AND OVERVIEW
by Tom Ball
Centerstream Publishing
Now on CD!
This exciting instructional book/CD pack features a comprehensive crash-course on all aspects of the blues harmonica, including: types of harps; buying a harmonica and breaking it in; maintenance and repair; breathing and phrasing; tablature; 12-bar blues; playing with a guitarist; non-standard tunings; and much more. Written in a fun and friendly conversational style – and only in tab notation – the book encourages players to learn at a comfortable pace, while developing their own style and feel. The accompanying CD includes demonstrations to inspire and aid players in practice.
00000159 Book/CD Pack $16.95
(0-93175-972-2)

THE SOURCEBOOK OF SONNY TERRY LICKS FOR HARMONICA
by Tom Ball
Centerstream Publications
"Sonny Terry has got to be explained to the people or his art will go over their head. By understanding Sonny Terry, you will learn how to enjoy and live in the real people's music that is on a train that's bound for glory." – Woody Guthrie, 1946.
This book/CD pack pays homage to Terry and his infamous playing. Besides 70 famous licks from Sonny, this pack gives you some quick harmonica lessons, information on Sonny's style, a discography with key chart, and a bibliography for future research. The CD includes each lick played out by the author.
_____00000178 Book/CD Pack $19.95

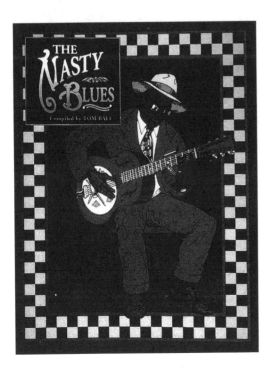

The Nasty Blues

Bawdy Blues Songs with Biographies, Lyrics & Guitar Chords
compiled by Tom Ball
Centerstream Publications

A celebration of crude and lewd songs by the best bluesmen and women in history, including Bo Carter, Bessie Smith, Irene Scruggs, Lil Johnson, Georgia White, Charlie Pickett, Lonnie Johnson, Ethel Waters, Tampa Red, and more. 30 songs in all: Sam, The Hot Dog Man • I Need A Little Sugar In My Bowl • Don't Mash My Digger So Deep • My Pencil Won't Write No More • Send Me A Man • Empty Bed Blues • One Hour Mama • and more. Includes cover art by Kevin Delaney, photos, and Robert Crumb illustrations throughout. ♪

$12.95 • 9 x 12 • 80 pages • Softcover • January •
0-93175-987-0 • HL00000049

GUITAR INSTRUCTION & TECHNIQUE

Guitar Chords Plus
by Ron Middlebrook
A comprehensive study of normal and extended chords, tuning, keys, transposing, capo use, and more. Includes over 500 helpful photos and diagrams, a key to guitar symbols, and a glossary of guitar terms.
00000011 ....$11.95

Guitar Tuning for the Complete Musical Idiot (For Smart People Too)*
by Ron Middlebrook
A complete book on how to tune up. Contents include: Everything You Need To Know About Tuning; Intonation; Strings; 12-String Tuning; Picks; and much more.
00000002 ....$5.95

Introduction to Roots Guitar   VHS
AN OVERVIEW OF NORTH AMERICAN FOLK STYLES
by Doug Cox
This book/CD pack by Canada's premier guitar and Dobro® player introduces beginning to intermediate players to many of the basics of folk/roots guitar. Topics covered include: basic theory, tuning, reading tablature, right- and left-hand patterns, blues rhythms, Travis picking, frailing patterns, flatpicking, open tunings, slide and many more–everything necessary to become a true roots guitar player! The CD includes 40 helpful demonstration tracks.
00000262 Book/CD Pack $17.95
Also available:
00000265 Video $19.95

Killer Pentatonics for Guitar*
by Dave Celentano
Covers innovative and diverse ways of playing pentatonic scales in blues, rock and heavy metal. The licks and ideas in this book will give you a fresh approach to playing the pentatonic scale, hopefully inspiring you to reach for higher levels in your playing. The 37-minute companion CD features recorded examples.
00000285 Book/CD Pack $17.95

Left Hand Guitar Chord Chart*
by Ron Middlebrook
Printed on durable card stock, this "first-of-a-kind" guitar chord chart displays all forms of major and minor chords in two forms, beginner and advanced.
00000005 ....$2.95

Melody Chords for Guitar*
by Allan Holdsworth
Influential fusion player Allan Holdsworth provides guitarists with a simplified method of learning chords, in diagram form, for playing accompaniments and for playing popular melodies in "chord-solo" style. Covers: major, minor, altered, dominant and diminished scale notes in chord form, with lots of helpful reference tables and diagrams.
00000222..$19.95

Modal Jams and Theory*
USING THE MODES FOR SOLO GUITAR
by Dave Celentano
This book shows you how to play the modes, the theory behind mode construction, how to play any mode in any key, how to play the proper mode over a given chord progression, and how to write chord progressions for each of the seven modes. The accompanying CD includes two rhythm tracks (drums, bass, keyboard and rhythm guitar), and a short solo for each mode so guitarists can practice their solos with a "real" band.
00000163 Book/CD Pack $17.95

Monster Scales and Modes*
by Dave Celentano
This book is a complete compilation of scales, modes, exotic scales, and theory. It covers the most common and exotic scales, theory on how they're constructed, and practical applications. No prior music theory knowledge is necessary, since every section is broken down and explained very clearly.
00000140..$7.95

Open Guitar Tunings*
by Ron Middlebrook
This booklet illustrates over 75 different tunings in easy-to-read diagrams. Includes tunings used by artists such as Chet Atkins, Michael Hedges, Jimmy Page, Joe Satriani and more for rock, blues, bluegrass, folk and country styles including open D (for slide guitar), Em, open C, modal tunings and many more.
00000130..$4.95

Open Tunings for Guitar*
by Dorian Michael
Seasoned guitar vet Dorian Michael provides 14 folk songs in 9 tunings to help guitarists become comfortable with changing tunings to expand their range. Songs are ordered so that changing from one tuning to another is logical and non-intrusive. Includes: Fisher Blues (DADGBE) • Fine Toast to Hewlett (DGDGBE) • George Barbazan (DGDGBD) • Amelia (DGDGCD) • Will the Circle Be Unbroken (DADF#AD) • more.
00000224 Book/CD Pack $19.95

Rock Rhythm Guitar
FOR ACOUSTIC & ELECTRIC GUITAR
by Dave Celentano
In this helpful book/CD pack, ace instructor Dave Celentano cuts out all the confusing technical talk and just gives guitarists the essential tools to get them playing. With his tips, anyone can build a solid foundation of basic skills to play almost any rhythm guitar style. The exercises and examples are all on the CD, and are laid out in order of difficulty, so players can master new techniques, then move on to more challenging material.
00000274 Book/CD Pack $17.95

Scales and Modes in the Beginning*
by Ron Middlebrook
The most comprehensive and complete scale book written especially for the guitar. Chapers include: Fretboard Visualization • Scale Terminology • Scales and Modes • and a Scale to Chord Guide.
00000010..$11.95

Slide Guitar and Open Tunings*
by Doug Cox
Explores the basics of open tunings and slide guitar for the intermediate player, including licks, chords, songs and patterns. This is not just a repertoire book, but rather an approach for guitarists to jam with others, invent their own songs, and understand how to find their way around open tunings with and without a slide. The accompanying CD features 37 tracks.
00000243 Book/CD Pack $17.95

Speed Metal
by Dave Celentano
In an attempt to teach the aspiring rock guitarist how to pick faster and play more melodically, Dave Celentano uses heavy metal neo-classical styles from Paganini and Bach to rock in this great new book/CD pack. The book is structured to take the player through the examples in order of difficulty, from easiest to most challenging.
00000261 Book/CD Pack $17.95

*Includes tablature